STEP-BY-STEP

50 Glorious Garnishes

STEP-BY-STEP

50 Glorious Garnishes

Janet Brinkworth

Photography by Karl Adamson

SMITHMARK

For Mum and Dad, with love and thanks.

This edition published in 1996 by
SMITHMARK Publishers
a division of U.S. Media Holdings, Inc.
16 East 32nd Street
New York
NY 10016

SMITHMARK books are available for bulk purchase for sales promotion
and premium use. For details write or call the Manager of Special Sales,
SMITHMARK Publishers
a division of U.S. Media Holdings, Inc.
16 East 32nd Street
New York
NY 10016
(212) 532 - 6600

ISBN 0 7651 9755 3

Publisher: Joanna Lorenz
Senior Cookery Editor: Linda Fraser
Cookery Editor: Maggie Mayhew
Copy Editor: Jenni Fleetwood
Designer: Lilian Lindblom
Photography: Karl Adamson
Assistant Home Economist: Zoë Kean
Stylist: Clare Hunt

Printed and bound in Hong Kong

CONTENTS

INTRODUCTION

Garnishing is probably the best way of transforming any recipe from the ordinary to the extraordinary, using the simplest ingredients with just a touch of effort and imagination. For example, take a simple dish of broiled chicken, add a few sprigs of thyme and several olives, and it is immediately transformed into a magical Mediterranean meal!

All sorts of ingredients can be used to garnish or decorate food – it is often a good idea to echo the main ingredients of the dish, but a colorful contrast can be just as effective. Opt for a classic, understated garnish, designed to subtly embellish the dish, or a gloriously over-the-top item such as red chilies tied together with raffia – a feast for the eye, not the palate. Garnishes are fun as well as functional and provide a marvelous opportunity for stamping your own personality on the food you serve.

Vegetables, herbs, fruit and flowers, whether real or craftily sculpted to imitate the original, may be used for garnishing. Chives are a favorite herb, thanks to their versatility. Not only can they be chopped or sliced but they can also be used as edible string for tying up bundles of herbs or vegetables.

Presentation is as important as preparation. Choose your crockery with care, selecting colors that enhance the food rather than clash with it. Avoid overpowering patterns unless the food is very plain. You don't have to be an accomplished artist to excel at garnishing. Some of the simplest effects can be stunning. Experiment to find the most pleasing arrangement, whether this is an elaborate decoration around the rim of a dish or merely a few carefully chosen garden flowers laid on top of a cake.

Equipment

It is not necessary to have a vast array of equipment or gadgets for making garnishes, but there are some items that will make the task infinitely easier.

Cannelle knife

This tool is great for carving stripes in the skin of citrus fruit. It is also good for decorating cucumbers, zucchini or any other soft-skinned vegetables. Pare off thin strips before slicing the fruit or vegetable, to make an attractive edge.

Cutters

A basic set of round cutters can be expanded gradually to include diamonds, squares, stars, hearts and flowers. Use them to cut out shapes from thinly sliced vegetables, slivers of red and green bell pepper or citrus peel. Look out for tiny aspic cutters in a variety of interesting shapes.

Knives

A small turning, or paring, knife is essential for carving out designs on fruit skins, such as melon, and also for fluting button mushrooms. A good sharp cook's knife or chopping knife, will make chopping herbs a simple job. Make sure you regularly sharpen knives to maintain the blades.

Melon baller

A handy little tool with either a large or small scoop at the end, this is used to make small balls of fruit or vegetables.

Pastry brushes

Buy good-quality brushes with tightly packed bristles. A normal paintbrush can be used, as long as the bristles are securely fixed, it is washed thoroughly before use and, of course, isn't used for painting!

Pastry bags and tips

A medium pastry bag with a selection of tips is very useful to have for garnishing sweet and savory dishes. Use small disposable pastry bags for chocolate or icing, where a fine line is required.

Raffia

An excellent standby for tying almost anything, raffia looks much more attractive than string. It is now available in all sorts of colors and can be bought in most florists or good garden stores.

Ribbon

Keep a small stock in various colors and widths for that final finishing touch. Use ribbon to tie around cold soufflé or mousse dishes or tie around garlands of fresh flowers or leaves to keep them in place.

Sieves

Both large and small sieves are essential items in any kitchen.

Skewers and toothpicks

Wooden and metal skewers can be used in a variety of ways, as can toothpicks. Drop spots of cream onto fruit sauces and use the point of a toothpick or skewer to drag the spots into heart or star shapes.

Small scissors

These are perfect for small garnishes where knives would be difficult to use. They are especially useful for cutting chives and other herbs.

Swivel-blade vegetable peelers

Both long-handled and broad-handled peelers can be used for much more than just peeling potatoes and carrots. Use to pare vegetables into thin strips before cooking.

Tea strainer

A tea strainer comes in handy for sifting confectioner's sugar over small items such as individual mousses and single servings of desserts.

Zester

Ideal for cucumbers and citrus fruit, a zester has the same function as a cannelle knife but produces a row of thin stripes.

metal skewers

toothpick

raffia

ribbon

wooden skewers

sieve

swivel-blade vegetable peelers

cannelle knife

zester

melon baller

tea strainer

cutters

scissors

knives

pastry bags and tips

pastry brushes

Pantry Standbys

A surprising number of garnishes can be made in advance and then stored for later use. Keep these items handy in a pantry or fridge and you should never have a problem in coming up with an instant garnish.

Chive braids
These can be made 1–2 days in advance and kept on damp paper towels in an airtight box in the fridge.

Chocolate curls and leaves
These can be made up to a month in advance and stored in a cool place on waxed paper in airtight containers.

Cinnamon sticks
Tie together long cinnamon sticks, using ribbon or raffia and store them in an airtight container. Place the tied bundles at the side of serving plates for an unusual touch.

Cookies
Sweet and savory cookies can be made ahead of time. Simply cut into shapes, bake and then store in airtight tins or freeze them. To use, thaw for half an hour, dust sweet cookies with confectioner's sugar and serve with mousses and fruit fools.

Cucumbers
Keep a cucumber in the vegetable drawer of your fridge and you'll find that you can always use it to rustle up a garnish in a matter of minutes.

Dried chilies
Large and small dried chilies look stunning in a bowl in the kitchen and are then readily available to use as a garnish tied together with a little raffia.

Fresh chilies
Bright red and green chilies make an attractive addition to Asian dishes. Use raffia to tie together bunches of chilies; add one or two sprigs of fresh herbs, if you like.

Fruit purées
Made in advance and frozen in ice cube trays, these are marvelous for decorating desserts. Thaw the cubes of fruit purée in the microwave or in a saucepan, swirl on a plate and top with the dessert.

Herb butter
Rolls of herb butter can be frozen, ready for slicing at a moment's notice. Serve on top of broiled meat, poultry or fish.

Herbs
The best herbs are home-grown, but purchased herbs will stay fresh in the fridge for 4–5 days. Trim the ends, wash and shake well, then place on damp paper towels in a storage box.

Lemons and limes
These fruits keep well, and with a few simple cuts can quickly be transformed into a variety of garnishes. They can be used for both sweet and savory dishes.

Oranges
These can be cut into wedges or slices, and the slices can then be turned into a cone or a twist, for a very colorful, edible garnish or decoration.

Parmesan cheese
Nothing lifts a plate of pasta more than a delicate curl of Parmesan, and a salad becomes special when topped with a few Parmesan shavings.

Radishes
Cut into roses using a small sharp knife or make zigzag cuts around the middle and pull apart to make Vandyke radishes. Radishes can also be left whole, with their leaves attached, to garnish a salad.

Red currant bunches
Drape bunches of red currants over sweet dishes, or tie two bunches together with long pieces of fresh chives.

raffia

fresh flowers

chocolate

oranges

herbs

radishes

fresh
chilies

dried chilies

lemons and
limes

Parmesan
cheese

cucumbers

cinnamon sticks

red currant
bunches

Simple Vegetable Garnishes

The vegetable most often used for garnishing is the cucumber. It can be cut and sliced in a wide variety of ways, some of which are described below, together with suggestions for using bell peppers, leeks, tomatoes and green beans

Bell pepper triangles

Cut 1 red and 1 yellow bell pepper into quarters and remove the seeds. Then cut out 2 x ¾ x ½-inch rectangles. Make a cut two-thirds of the way into the short side, three-quarters of the way up. Turn the piece of pepper 180° and repeat. Twist the pepper and pull to form a triangle. Alternate the red and yellow triangles around the rim of a plate, as a border, or use just one or two as a garnish for individual servings.

Cucumber

• Spirals – cut two slices, each ⅛-inch thick. Make a cut from the center to the edge on both slices. Twist each slice into an "S" shape. Place the spirals next to each other and link them together.
• Border – cut six slices, each ⅛-inch thick, then cut each slice in half. Place around the rim of the plate, arranging alternate slices skin-side inwards and skin-side outwards.
• Fan – cut a cucumber into 2-inch lengths. Then cut each piece in half lengthwise. Make six or seven very fine cuts three-quarters of the way into the cucumber half. Press down gently and fan out the slices.

Green beans

Slice beans at an angle into ¾-inch lengths. Sprinkle over salads or use in pairs to make a cross on top of a canapé.

Leek curls

Cut a leek into 2-inch lengths, then slice in half lengthwise. Cut the leek strips into fine matchsticks. Put them in a bowl of iced water and chill for about two hours or until they form tight curls. Drain the curls before using them.

Mushrooms

Use a small sharp knife to cut small grooves in a spiral around the caps of button mushrooms, Use these "turned" mushrooms raw or cook them lightly in butter until golden. Place a few on each diner's plate to thrill and impress your guests.

Radishes

Make zigzag cuts around the middle and pull apart to make Vandyke radishes. Use with the fresh green leaves still intact, to brighten up salads and many other cold dishes.

Scallions

Use a small sharp knife to cut the green ends of scallions into fine long shreds that are still attached to the white part. Plunge the scallions into iced water and let sit overnight to allow the ends to curl up. This can also be done with shorter lengths of shredded scallion. Use these curly shreds to sprinkle over salads and hot savory dishes.

Tomato bowl

Using a small sharp knife cut a "V" into the middle of a large firm tomato, inserting the knife right through to the center. Make identical cuts all the way around the tomato so that it looks as though a zigzag line has been drawn around it. Gently pull the tomato apart and top each half with two quarter slices of cucumber and a parsley sprig.

radishes

tomato bowl

leek curls

green beans

cucumber fan

cucumber spirals

*bell
pepper triangles*

*large
cucumber
fan*

cucumber border

Using Fruit and Flowers

Some of the most eye-catching garnishes and decorations are made from fruit and flowers.

Baby rose posy

Choose six perfect small roses and trim the stems to about 1 inch. Place five of the roses in a ring on a cake so that the stems meet in the center. Place the remaining rose on top to finish the posy.

Edible flowers

Edible flowers, such as nasturtiums, can be used to enliven a salad or a scoop of ice cream. Simply scatter several across the plate. Both blue and white borage flowers look stunning in salads and drinks during the summer months.

Flower bouquet

Gather some fresh flowers together in a bouquet, tie with some raffia or a ribbon and place on top of a cake.

Lemon basket

Holding a lemon lengthwise, cut it in half around the middle to within ¼ inch of the center. Make an identical cut on the opposite side of the lemon. Slice down from the top to meet the first incision, then make a similar cut from the top to the second incision. Pull the loose segments away and discard. Cut out the flesh under the "handle" and discard it. Put a sprig of dill in the center of the lemon basket and place on a dish of canapés or use to garnish a large, whole, cooked fish.

Lemon wedges

Cut a lemon lengthwise in half, then cut each half into three wedges. Carefully remove any seeds. Arrange the wedges on the plate in pairs, separated by a sprig of parsley. Use a lime instead, if you prefer.

Lime segments

Peel a lime, making sure that you remove all the pith. Separate into neat segments, cutting between each of the membranes. Place the segments in pairs, and arrange a little watercress on top.

Melon bowl

Insert a small sharp knife halfway down a cantaloupe at an angle and push it in as far as the center. Cut a series of deep "V" shapes all the way around the melon until you get back to where you started. Gently pull the melon apart and turn one half upright. Remove the seeds from both halves. Using a melon baller, scoop the flesh of one half into small balls and place these into the cavity of the other half.

Orange flower

Cut two thin slices from an orange, then cut each slice in half. Cut along the inside of the pith on one half to within ⅛ inch of the end. Turn the strip of rind in, to form a loop on top of the half-slice. Repeat with the remaining half-slices. Place them in a ring with the loops on the outside.

Pear fan

Peel a pear, leaving the stem intact. Poach in a light syrup until tender. Cut in half lengthwise. Place cut-side down on a chopping board and cut about eight thin slices, leaving then intact at the top. Press down gently to fan the slices apart.

Strawberry fan

Make a strawberry into a fan by cutting into thin slices, from the pointed end, almost to the top. Leave the strawberry hull and calyx in place and gently fan out the strawberry slices. Make half strawberry fans by halving the strawberry first and then placing the cut side down on a board. Make cuts from the leaf end almost to the pointed end and fan out gently.

lemon basket

lemon wedges

lime segments

fresh flowers

orange flower

flower bouquet

pear fan

strawberry
fan

baby rose
posy

melon bowl

TECHNIQUES

Preparing ingredients is easy when you follow
these step-by-step instructions.

Cutting Carrot Julienne

It may seem a little time-consuming and fussy
to cut vegetables into thin julienne strips, but the
result is definitely worth it.

1 Peel a carrot and take a thin slice off each side to square it up.
Cut into 2-inch lengths.

2 Cut each of the lengths into
¼ inch thick slices.

3 Stack the slices and cut these into
fine matchsticks to form julienne.

Making a Radish Rose

This is a classic garnish. The technique can also
be applied to the bulb of a salad onion or a baby
turnip. Radish roses can be made in advance and
kept in water in the fridge for up to three days.

1 Carefully trim both ends of the
radish, removing the root and stalk.

2 Place base-end down and cut in
half vertically, stopping the knife just
before it reaches the base. Repeat until
the radish looks as though it has been
cut into eight equal segments, but is in
fact held together at the base.

3 Put the radish in a bowl of ice water and let sit for at least 4 hours to open up.

Blanching

Blanching is a method of partial cooking, where foods are immersed in boiling water or boiled briefly. In terms of garnishing, the technique is used to make vegetables, fruit and herbs more pliable and easier to handle. It also helps to preserve a bright color.

1 Fill a large saucepan with water and bring to a boil. Add the prepared vegetable or fruit for the time suggested in each individual recipe: 1–2 minutes is usually ample.

2 Drain well in a strainer, then refresh in cold water. Change the water once or twice, as necessary, until the food is completely cold. Drain again.

3 Blanched vegetables and fruit can be used in various ways: stamped out into diamonds, perhaps, or tied in a bundle with a wilted chive.

Peeling Tomatoes

It only takes a few moments to peel tomatoes, but the difference this makes to a dish is amazing. Concassing tomatoes (chopping them into neat squares) adds the finishing touch.

1 Make a small cross in the skin on the base of each tomato. Use a small sharp knife to cut out the calyx.

2 Place the tomatoes in boiling water for 20–30 seconds, drain and refresh under cold water. Gently peel off the loosened skin.

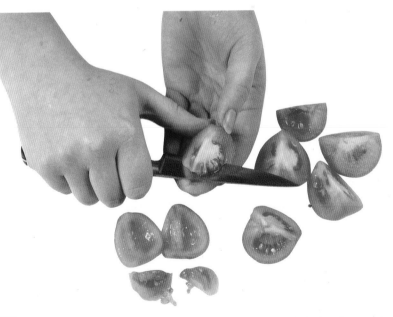

3 Cut the tomatoes into quarters. Place each tomato quarter flesh-side down and slide a knife along the inner flesh, scooping out all the seeds. Cut the flesh into neat ¼-inch squares.

Piping

Piping is an art that anyone can master with a bit of practice. It is widely used as a form of decoration, for shaping cookies, creating a decorative border with mashed potatoes or making attractively shaped meringues.

Melting Chocolate

Melting chocolate takes a little patience and care, but the process is very simple. It can be done over hot water or in a microwave oven.

1 Select the right tip – a star for a rosette, for instance, or a small plain tip for writing. Half-fill the pastry bag, then twist it closed, at the same time forcing out any air.

2 Hold the bag firmly in one hand, with your fingers around the twisted section. Use the other hand to lightly guide the tip. Exert a very firm, steady pressure and start to pipe. The trick is to keep the pressure steady until the design is finished. A sudden squeeze will produce a large blob rather than an even flow.

1 To microwave, break 4 ounces semisweet chocolate into squares or chop it into small pieces. Place in a heat-proof bowl and cook on medium (50% power) for 2 minutes. Sweet and white chocolate should be melted for the same time, but on low (30% power).

2 To melt chocolate over hot water, bring a small saucepan of water to a boil. Turn off the heat and place the bowl of chocolate over the hot water. The bowl must not touch the water nor should any drops of water be allowed to fall into the chocolate, or it will become grainy.

3 As soon as the design is complete, stop applying pressure, push down slightly and quickly lift up the tip.

3 Leave the chocolate until very soft, then stir it lightly. Melted chocolate can be used in many ways: spooned into paper pastry bags and piped, drizzled over tiny cupcakes or mixed with a little cream and spread over a cake as an icing.

Frosting

Frosting is a classic decoration, usually used for fruit or flowers. Try arranging frosted grapes on a cheesecake, or scatter frosted rose petals around a delicate lemon mousse. Whole roses can also be decorated in this way.

1 Separate the petals of a rose, or cut grapes into small bunches . Whisk an egg white until it starts to become foamy. Brush gently onto each of the rose petals or grapes, covering them completely.

2 Sprinkle superfine sugar onto a sheet of waxed paper. Place the rose petals or grapes on the sheet and sprinkle over more sugar, then toss lightly until completely covered.

3 Place the rose petals or grapes on a wire rack and allow to dry completely for several hours.

Stenciling

Stenciling can be a fun way to liven up sponge cakes, cookies or even a soufflé! There are no hard and fast rules – experiment with different templates such as lacy paper doilies.

1 Place a cake on a sheet of waxed paper. Cut out strips of paper and lay these in a random criss-cross pattern across the cake. Dust with confectioner's sugar, then carefully remove the paper strips to reveal the pattern.

2 For a two-tone effect, dust a cake with confectioner's sugar, covering it completely. Place a doily lightly over the cake and dust with cocoa powder. Lift off carefully.

3 Cut a small design or initial out of cardboard and place it over a cookie. Dust the cookie with confectioner's sugar or cocoa powder before removing the cardboard.

Petal Sushi with Chili Flowers

Make these chili flowers several hours before needed to allow the "flowers" to open up fully.

Makes 24

INGREDIENTS
3 tablespoons rice wine vinegar
2 tablespoons superfine sugar
½ teaspoon salt
1¼ cups jasmine rice, cooked
  and still warm
4–8 asparagus spears, trimmed
1 tablespoon wasabi (hot green
  horseradish)
1 tablespoon pickled ginger,
  thinly sliced
4 toasted nori sheets
4 red chilies, to garnish

wasabi

rice wine

red chilies

jasmine rice

asparagus spears

toasted nori

superfine sugar

COOK'S TIP
Wear rubber gloves or wash your hands thoroughly after handling chilies – they can irritate the skin badly.

1 Start by making the garnish. Use a small pair of scissors or a slim-bladed knife to cut a chili carefully lengthwise up from the tip to within ½ inch of the stem end. Repeat this at regular intervals around the chili – more cuts will produce more petals. Repeat with the remaining chilies.

4 Cook the asparagus in boiling water until just tender. Drain, refresh in cold water and pat dry. Spread a little wasabi over each asparagus spear until thinly coated. Fold the pickled ginger slices around the asparagus.

2 Rinse the chilies in cold water and remove all the seeds. Place the chilies in a bowl of ice water and chill for at least 4 hours. For very curly flowers, leave the chilies overnight.

3 Place the rice, wine vinegar, sugar and salt in a small saucepan and heat gently until the sugar has dissolved. Pour the rice wine mixture over the rice and fold in, using a cutting action to mix evenly. Allow the mixture to cool.

5 Place a nori sheet on a bamboo rolling mat. Leaving a ½-inch border all around, use wet hands to spread about a quarter of the cooked rice evenly across the nori. Place one or two wasabi-coated asparagus spears widthwise across the center of the rice. Pick up the corners of the mat and roll up the nori to enclose the filling in a neat cylinder. Press one side of the cylinder flat to produce a petal shape. Pat the ends gently to seal in the rice. Make three more cylinders in the same way, then cut each cylinder into six neat slices. Arrange the petal sushi on a platter and garnish with the drained chili flowers. Serve with pickled ginger and a chili dipping sauce

Wild Rice Blinis with Vegetable Shreds

The vegetable shreds – baby julienne strips – can be arranged to form little haystacks on each blini or simply piled randomly; either way, you'll find it produces a stunning result.

Makes 40

INGREDIENTS
scant 1½ cups wholewheat flour
1¼ cups sour cream
½ cup wild rice
2 eggs, beaten
2 tablespoons butter, melted
1 teaspoon baking powder
2 teaspoons baking soda
1 tablespoon hot water
oil, for frying
salt and freshly ground black
   pepper
1 cup crème fraîche, to serve

FOR THE GARNISH
1 each red, yellow and green
   peppers, seeded and
   quartered
1 carrot, peeled
½ cucumber

1 Put the flour in a bowl. Gradually add the sour cream, mixing until smooth. Cover and chill for at least 2 hours. Meanwhile, boil the wild rice in plenty of water for 45–50 minutes until slightly overcooked. Drain, rinse under cold water, then drain again. Set aside.

2 Make the garnish. Cut the red and yellow bell peppers, the carrot and the cucumber into julienne strips ¾-inch long and ¼-inch wide. Cover and chill until they are required.

3 Preheat the oven to 275°F. Line a baking sheet with waxed paper. Beat the eggs, butter and baking powder into the flour mixture. Mix the baking soda with the hot water and stir into the batter with the rice.

4 Add a little salt and pepper to the batter. Heat a little oil in a heavy-bottomed frying pan, then drop in small spoonfuls of the rice batter. Cook until bubbles appear on the surface of each blini and they become firm. Flip the blinis over and cook the other side briefly. Stack on the prepared baking sheet and keep warm in the oven. Repeat with the remaining batter. Serve the blinis warm, topped with crème fraîche. Garnish each blini with the vegetable shreds.

butter
baking powder
oil
sour cream
wild rice
crème fraîche
wholewheat flour
eggs
baking soda
red and yellow bell peppers
cucumber
carrot

Chili Shrimp in Cucumber Cups on a Herb-rimmed Plate

Try garnishing the rim of the plate rather than the food itself – a very simple but stunning idea.

Makes 20–24

INGREDIENTS
4 small red chilies, seeded and
  finely diced
2 teaspoons finely grated
  fresh ginger
1 large garlic clove, crushed
3 tablespoons light soy sauce
8 ounces cooked shrimp,
  peeled and deveined
2 cucumbers

FOR THE GARNISH
1 tablespoon butter, softened
2 tablespoons chopped fresh
  chives

shrimp

garlic

chives

butter   *red chilies*

cucumber

soy sauce   *fresh ginger*

COOK'S TIP
Use any type of chopped herb or, for a more colorful edge, dust with chili powder or ground turmeric.

1 Combine the chilies, ginger, garlic and soy sauce in a bowl. Add the shrimp and toss them in the marinade. Cover and chill for 2–4 hours.

2 Trim both ends of the cucumbers, then cut them into ¾-inch lengths. Use a 1¼-inch round aspic cutter to stamp out rounds, and discard the skin.

3 Using a melon baller, scoop out the cucumber seeds to make little cups. Place upside-down on paper towels to drain for 20–30 minutes.

4 Brush the butter around the rim of the plate. Sprinkle the chives over the butter to form a decorative edge. Tip the plate and shake lightly to remove any loose chives. Arrange the cucumber cups in the center of the plate and fill each with 2–3 marinated shrimp.

Poppadums with Caviar and Chopped Egg

An unusual way of serving caviar – topped with a garnish of chopped hard-cooked egg.

Makes 24

INGREDIENTS
6 ready-to-cook poppadums
1 ounce caviar or black
   lumpfish roe
2 hard-cooked eggs, to garnish

poppadums

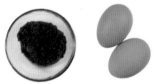

caviar   *eggs*

1 Preheat the broiler to high. Cut the poppadums carefully into quarters, using a pair of kitchen scissors.

2 Place several poppadum quarters on a foil-lined broiler pan. Watching all the time, broil for 5–10 seconds or until they have turned white and have curled up. Remove, then repeat with the remaining poppadums. Store in an airtight container for up to 3 days.

3 Shell the eggs and cut them in half. Scoop the yolks into a strainer and set aside. Chop the whites very finely.

4 Using the back of a spoon, rub the reserved egg yolk through the strainer into a small bowl. Place a small spoonful of caviar or lumpfish roe on one corner of each poppadum. Top with a small amount of egg white and then a dot of egg yolk. Serve at once.

Baby Ginger Rösti with Chili Bouquets

Chilies make a wonderfully versatile garnish – even a single chili placed on the side of a plate can set off a dish.

Makes 20–24

INGREDIENTS
1 pound potatoes
2 tablespoons grated fresh ginger
1 tablespoon all-purpose flour
oil, for frying
salt and freshly ground black pepper

FOR THE GARNISH
2 large red chilies
raffia, for tying
large sprigs of parsley or cilantro (optional)

raffia

potatoes

all-purpose flour

oil

red chilies

fresh ginger

parsley

1 Preheat the oven to 275°F. Line a baking sheet with paper towels. Peel the potatoes and grate them coarsely into a bowl. Stir in the fresh ginger. Add the flour, salt and pepper, then mix together well.

3 Fry the rösti for 2–3 minutes on each side until golden brown.

2 Heat a little oil in a non-stick frying pan, then gently drop in a few small spoonfuls of the coarsely grated potato mixture.

4 Place on the prepared baking sheet and keep warm in the oven. Make more rösti in the same way.

5 To make the garnish, tie the stems of the chilies together with a small piece of raffia. For an interesting color contrast, add a large sprig of parsley or cilantro. Arrange the rösti on a plate, set the chilies on the rim and serve.

Smoked Mackerel Pâté with Lemon Twists

Linking several lemon twists together with a sprig of parsley creates a simple but effective result.

Makes 40 – 50

INGREDIENTS
12 slices wholewheat bread
9 ounces smoked mackerel
  fillets, skinned
½ cup cream cheese
½ cup strained plain yogurt
5 teaspoons horseradish cream
1 teaspoon paprika

FOR THE GARNISH
1 lemon
sprig of parsley

parsley

cream cheese

strained plain yogurt

smoked mackerel fillets

horseradish cream

paprika

wholewheat bread

lemon

1 Preheat the oven to 300°F. Using a small round cutter, stamp out rounds of wholewheat bread.

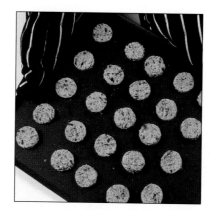

2 Place on a baking sheet and place in the oven. Bake for 30 – 40 minutes until hard and lightly golden. Place on a rack to cool. These can be made in advance and stored in an airtight tin for up to a week.

3 Place the smoked mackerel, cream cheese, yogurt and horseradish into a food processor. Process until smooth.

4 Place the pâté in a pastry bag fitted with a star tip and pipe a small rosette onto each toast. Dust each one with a little paprika.

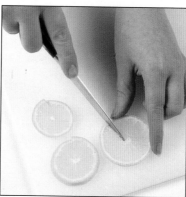

5 To make the garnish, use a sharp knife to cut the lemon into ¼-inch slices. Make a cut in each slice from the center out to the skin.

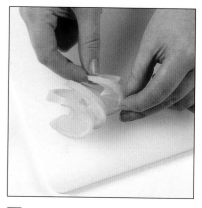

6 Hold the slice either side of the cut and twist to form an "S" shape. Place three together and place a sprig of parsley under one end slice.

Broiled Pears and Stilton with a Gilded Pear

Gilding is a stunning way to finish a dish. Any fruit can be transformed like this and even used as an unusual table decoration.

Makes 24

INGREDIENTS
4 large ripe eating pears
1 cup Stilton cheese
2 tablespoons strained plain
  yogurt
salt and freshly ground black
  pepper

FOR THE GARNISH
1 small pear, preferably
  with stalk intact
1 book edible gold leaf

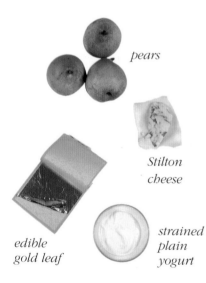

pears

Stilton cheese

edible gold leaf

strained plain yogurt

1 Make the garnish. Stand the small pear upright. If the base is particularly rounded, you may find it necessary to trim about ¼ inch off the bottom of the pear so that it remains level.

2 Tear off pieces of gold leaf and press over the pear, smoothing the leaf on carefully until the pear is covered evenly. Set aside.

3 Preheat the broiler to high. Line a broiler pan with foil. Cut the large pears lengthwise into thick slices on either side of the core. Using a small diamond aspic cutter, stamp out about 24 diamonds of pear and place in the prepared broiler pan.

4 Crumble the Stilton into a bowl. Stir in the yogurt to make a creamy paste, then add salt and pepper to taste. Place a teaspoonful of the mixture on each pear diamond. Broil until the Stilton starts to melt and bubble. Arrange on a platter with the gilded pear and serve immediately.

Egg and Tomato Tartlets with a Quail's Egg Nest

Quail's eggs make a delightful garnish with their pretty shells left on. Hard-cook a few to use as an edible garnish, but shell before eating.

Makes 24

INGREDIENTS
24 cooked tartlet cases
24 quail's eggs
6 cherry tomatoes
24 parsley sprigs
salt and freshly ground
   black pepper

FOR THE GARNISH
12 quail's eggs
2 leeks, trimmed

quail's eggs

*cherry
tomatoes*

leek

*tartlet
cases*

parsley

1 Preheat the oven to 350°F. Season the tartlet shells and place them on baking sheets. Carefully break the quail's eggs into a bowl, taking care to keep the yolks intact. Cut the cherry tomatoes into quarters.

2 Spoon a yolk into each tartlet. Add a small amount of egg white to each, but do not overfill. Place a tomato quarter in each tartlet. Cover with foil and bake for 10–12 minutes until just set. Top each one with a parsley sprig.

3 Make the garnish. Place the quail's eggs in a saucepan of cold water, bring to a boil, cover and remove from the heat. Let sit for 6–8 minutes. Drain the eggs and refresh under cold running water until they are cool. Drain and pat the shells dry.

4 Shred the leeks finely by hand or with a food processor fitted with a fine shredding plate. Form the shredded leeks into a nest on a large platter, with the hard-cooked quail's eggs nestled on top. Add the warm egg and tomato tartlets and serve.

Potato Blinis with Dill Cream and Smoked Salmon Roses

A rose of smoked salmon complements fluffy potato blinis perfectly and provides an interesting combination of flavors and textures.

Serves 8

INGREDIENTS
3 potatoes, peeled and
  quartered
3 eggs, beaten
4 tablespoons self-rising flour
⅔ cup heavy cream
2 egg whites
1 teaspoon grated nutmeg
oil, for frying
salt and freshly ground black
  pepper
4 tablespoons dill mustard and
  1¼ cups sour cream,
  to serve

TO GARNISH
8 smoked salmon slices
sprigs of dill

smoked salmon

heavy cream

potatoes

eggs

nutmeg

dill mustard

sour cream

self-rising flour

1 Cook the potatoes in boiling lightly salted water until tender. Drain, return to the saucepan and place over low heat to steam-dry and drive off any excess moisture. Pass through a food mill (or press through a strainer with a wooden spoon) into a bowl. Mash lightly, then cool, cover and chill. Mix the dill mustard and sour cream in a bowl, cover and set aside.

2 Whisk the eggs and flour into the chilled mashed potatoes. Bring the heavy cream to a boil in a small pan, then whisk into the potato mixture until it forms a batter. Whisk the egg whites in a clean bowl until stiff peaks form. Gently fold these into the potato batter. Season with nutmeg, salt and pepper, then set aside.

3 Make the garnish. Fold one slice of smoked salmon lengthwise in half. Holding one end with finger and thumb, start rolling the salmon around on itself to form a loose pinwheel.

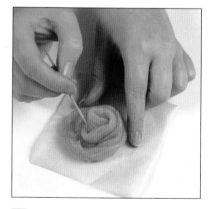

4 Set the salmon rose on the work surface and gently pinch the base to hold it together. Using a toothpick or small knife, gently separate each layer to form petals. Use the remaining smoked salmon to make more roses in the same way. Cover and chill.

5 Preheat the oven to 275°F. Line a baking sheet with waxed paper. Heat a little oil in a small nonstick frying pan or crêpe pan. Ladle in about ½ inch batter. Cook until golden and bubbles have started to form on top. Flip and cook the other side until golden.

6 Slide the blini onto the prepared baking sheet and keep warm in the oven. Make eight more blinis in the same way, greasing the pan with a little oil each time. Serve the blinis warm, topping each one with a spoonful of dill cream and a smoked salmon rose.

Thai Vichyssoise with Chive Braids

Give a classic French recipe an Asian slant and serve it topped with edible braids of chives.

Serves 6

INGREDIENTS

4 tablespoons butter
4 leeks, trimmed and thinly sliced
2 onions, thinly sliced
2 tablespoons Thai green curry paste
2 kaffir lime leaves
12 ounces floury potatoes, peeled and diced
4 cups vegetable stock
2 x 14-ounce cans unsweetened coconut milk
1 tablespoon fish sauce
30–60 thick chives, about 8 inches long, to garnish

onion

coconut milk

fish sauce

butter

Thai green curry paste

leek

chives

potato

kaffir lime leaves

1 Melt the butter in a large saucepan. Add the leeks, onions, curry paste and lime leaves. Stir to mix, then cover and cook for 15 minutes until the onions are tender but not colored.

2 Add the potatoes, stock and coconut milk. Bring to a boil, lower the heat, cover and simmer for about 25–30 minutes or until the potatoes are tender. Remove the lime leaves.

3 Purée the mixture in batches in a blender or pass through a food mill. Return to the clean pan and season with the fish sauce. Set aside.

4 Make the garnish. Pick out three of the thickest chives and two that are slightly thinner. Align the thicker chives on a work surface with a small bowl on one end to hold them still. Carefully braid the chives together to within 1 inch of the end.

5 Tie one of the thinner chives around the exposed end of the braid, then remove the bowl or board and tie the other end in the same way. Trim the ends of the ties and braids neatly with kitchen shears. Make five to eleven more braids in the same way.

6 Place the braids in a bowl and pour boiling water over them. Let stand for 20–30 seconds then drain and refresh under cold water. Drain again. Reheat the soup or serve it chilled, with one or two of the chive braids floating on the top.

Prosciutto Salad with an Avocado Fan

Avocados are amazingly versatile – they can serve as edible containers, be sliced or diced in a salad, or form the foundation of a delicious soup or sauce. However, they are at their most elegant when sliced thinly and fanned on a plate.

Serves 4

INGREDIENTS
3 avocados
1 cup prosciutto
1–2 bunches arugula
24 marinated black olives, drained

FOR THE DRESSING
1 tablespoon balsamic vinegar
1 teaspoon lemon juice
1 teaspoon prepared English mustard
1 teaspoon sugar
5 tablespoons olive oil
salt and freshly ground black pepper

prosciutto

arugula

avocados

English mustard

olive oil

black olives

lemon

1 Make the dressing by combining the balsamic vinegar, lemon juice, mustard and sugar in a bowl. Whisk in the oil, season to taste, and set aside.

2 Cut two avocados in half. Remove the pits and skin, and cut into ½-inch slices. Toss with half the dressing. Place the prosciutto, avocado and arugula on four plates. Sprinkle the olives and the remaining dressing over the salads.

3 Make the garnish. Halve, pit and peel the remaining avocado. Slice each half lengthwise into quarters. Gently draw a cannelle knife across the quarters at ½-inch intervals, to create regular stripes.

4 Make four cuts lengthwise down each avocado quarter leaving ½ inch intact at the end. Carefully fan out the slices and arrange on the plate.

Jumbo Shrimp with Salsa Verde and Lime

Limes are wonderfully versatile and look great simply cut into pieces, then dusted with a little finely chopped cilantro or parsley.

Serves 4

INGREDIENTS
½ cup white wine
2 teaspoons grated fresh ginger
2 teaspoons crushed garlic
24 raw jumbo shrimp, peeled and heads left intact
2 limes and 1 tablespoon chopped fresh cilantro, to garnish

FOR THE SALSA VERDE
1 small onion, quartered
1 bunch cilantro
1 teaspoon crushed garlic
6 tablespoons olive oil

fresh ginger

onion

jumbo shrimp

white wine

garlic

olive oil

lime

cilantro

1 Combine the white wine, ginger and garlic in a medium bowl. Add the shrimp, turning to coat them in the marinade. Cover and chill for 4–6 hours.

2 Make the salsa. Chop the onion coarsely in a food processor. Add the cilantro and garlic and process until finely chopped. With the motor running, pour in the oil through the feeder tube of the processor. When the salsa is thick and creamy, scrape it into a serving bowl. Preheat the broiler and line the broiler pan with foil.

3 Place half the shrimp on the broiler pan and cook for 5–6 minutes, turning them over halfway through cooking. Repeat with the remaining shrimp. Divide the shrimp among four plates. Cut the limes in half lengthwise, then into wedges. Press the long edge of each wedge into the chopped cilantro. Place two wedges on each plate. Serve with the salsa verde.

Smoked Salmon Terrine with Lemons

Lemons can be cut and sliced in so many ways. This smoked salmon terrine gives a time-honored accompaniment an intriguing new twist.

Serves 6

INGREDIENTS
4 sheets leaf gelatin
4 tablespoons water
14 ounces smoked salmon, sliced
1½ cups cream cheese
½ cup sour cream
2 tablespoons dill mustard
juice of 1 lime

FOR THE GARNISH
2 lemons
piece of muslin
raffia, for tying

raffia

cream cheese

lime

smoked salmon

leaf gelatin

dill mustard

lemons

sour cream

1 Soak the gelatin in the water in a small bowl, until softened. Meanwhile, line a one-pound loaf pan with clear plastic. Use some of the smoked salmon to line the pan, laying the slices widthwise across the bottom and up the sides, and leaving enough overlap to fold over the top of the filling.

2 Set aside enough of the remaining smoked salmon to make a middle layer the length of the pan. Chop the rest finely by hand or in a food processor. Beat together the cream cheese, crème fraîche and dill mustard with the chopped smoked salmon until everything is well combined.

3 Squeeze out the gelatin and melt gently in a small saucepan with the lime juice. Add to the smoked salmon mixture and mix thoroughly. Spoon half the mixture into the lined pan. Lay the reserved smoked salmon slices across the mixture, then spoon on the rest of the filling and smooth the top.

4 Tap the pan on the work surface to force out any trapped air. Fold over the overhanging salmon slices to cover the top. Cover with clear plastic and chill for at least 4 hours.

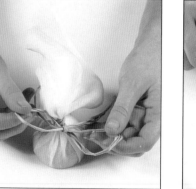

5 Make the garnish. Cut 1 lemon in half widthwise. Wrap each half in a square of muslin. Gather the muslin at the rounded end of the lemon and tie neatly with raffia.

6 Cut a small "V" from the side of the remaining lemon. Repeat ¼ inch further down. Repeat. Turn out the terrine, slice. Garnish with muslin-wrapped lemons and lemon leaves.

Crab Charlottes with Scallion Brushes

Scallion brushes are traditionally served with Chinese food but make an equally effective garnish for these crab charlottes.

Serves 4

INGREDIENTS
11 scallions
scant 1 cup butter, melted
8 slices white bread, crusts
  removed
11 ounces drained, canned or
  fresh boiled crab meat
salt and freshly ground
  black pepper

butter

crab meat

scallions

white bread

COOK'S TIP
Prepared in this way, scallions are perfect for brushing a marinade over barbecued food. They can also be served with crisp duck and Chinese pancakes, and used to dip in the hoisin sauce.

1 Start by making the garnish. Trim 8 of the scallions, removing the roots and bulbs. Cut off the tops at an angle to give a total length of about 6 inches.

4 Using a cookie cutter, stamp out rounds from the bread to fit the bottom and top of the molds. Cut the remaining bread into ¾-inch strips, and trim to the height of the molds.

2 Using a fine-bladed knife make 2-inch lengthwise cuts in the white part of a scallion. Keep the cuts parallel and as close together as possible. Prepare the remaining trimmed scallions in the same way. Place them in a bowl of ice water and chill for at least 4 hours until beautifully curled.

5 Dip the bread rounds for the bases in melted butter and drop into the molds. Dip the bread fingers in butter and use to line the sides.

3 Preheat the oven to 400°F. Chop the remaining scallions and cook in 1 tablespoon of the butter for 3–4 minutes until soft. Allow to cool. Use a little of the remaining butter to grease four large dariole molds.

6 Mix the crab meat with the cooked scallions. Season, then use to fill each mold. Dip the remaining bread rounds in butter and put on top. Bake on a baking sheet for 20 minutes. Turn out and garnish each with two brushes.

Tomato Soup with Swirled Cream

A swirl of cream is the classic finish for tomato soup. The technique is simplicity itself and works equally well on a savory or sweet sauce.

Serves 8

INGREDIENTS
1 tablespoon olive oil
2 onions, chopped
1 large floury potato, peeled and chopped
6–7 large flavorful tomatoes, peeled, seeded and chopped
3¾ cups vegetable stock
1 bunch basil, coarsely chopped
¾ cup sour cream
salt and freshly ground black pepper
⅔ cup light cream, to garnish

basil

onion

sour cream

tomatoes

potato

light cream

olive oil

1 Heat the olive oil in a large saucepan, add the onions, cover and cook over low heat for 10 minutes. Add the potato, replace the lid and cook for 5 minutes more. Stir in the tomatoes and vegetable stock.

2 Bring to a boil, then simmer for 35–40 minutes. Add the basil and seasoning. Purée in a food processor, then return to a clean pan and whisk in the sour cream. Heat without boiling, then ladle into warm soup bowls.

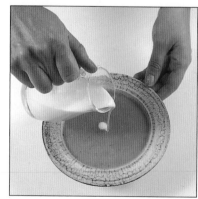

3 Pour the cream into a cup with a good pouring lip. Pour a swirl onto the surface of each bowl of soup.

4 Draw the tip of a fine skewer quickly backward and forward through the cream to create a pattern.

Chicken Liver Pâté with Tomato Finger Fans

Tomato fans make an unusual garnish for this delicious pâté.

Serves 6

INGREDIENTS
2 tablespoons olive oil
1 onion, chopped
1 tablespoon chopped fresh
  thyme
8 ounces chicken livers,
  trimmed
½ cup ruby port
½ cup heavy cream
salt and freshly ground
  black pepper

FOR THE GARNISH
5 firm tomatoes
flat-leaf parsley sprigs

chicken livers

heavy cream

ruby port

olive oil

tomatoes   *onion*

parsley   *thyme*

1 Heat the oil in a frying pan. Add the onion and thyme and sauté for 5 minutes, then cover and cook for 10 minutes. Add the chicken livers and sauté for 4–5 minutes until brown but still slightly soft. Remove the chicken livers. Stir the ruby port into the pan and cook until reduced by half.

2 Purée the chicken livers and wine mixture in a food processor or blender until smooth. Cool. Whip the cream to soft peaks and fold into the purée. Season to taste. Spoon the pâté into a serving dish; smooth the top. Chill for at least 3 hours.

3 Make the garnish. Cut the tomatoes into quarters. Hold each quarter skin-side down and use the knife to scoop out the pulp and seeds.

4 Make four cuts down the length of each tomato quarter, leaving about ½ inch intact at the top. Turn the tomato over and fan out the fingers. Top each tomato fan with a sprig of parsley. Serve a portion of pâté garnished with tomato fans.

Tarragon Chicken with Caramelized Onions

Served with slivers of herb butter, this makes a meal fit for any special celebration.

Serves 4

INGREDIENTS
4 skinless, boneless chicken
    breasts, about 6 ounces each
2 onions, thinly sliced
2 garlic cloves, crushed
4 tablespoons chopped fresh
    tarragon
juice of 2 oranges
3 tablespoons sunflower oil
1 tablespoon light brown sugar
4 tablespoons white wine
scant ½ cup butter
salt and freshly ground black
    pepper

FOR THE HERB BUTTER
½ cup butter, softened
4 tablespoons orange juice
4 tablespoons chopped fresh
    tarragon

butter

white wine

onions

oranges

light brown sugar

garlic

tarragon

sunflower oil

chicken breasts

1 First, make the herb butter. Put the butter in a bowl. Gradually beat in the orange juice, then add the tarragon. Cut a 10 x 8-inch piece of waxed paper. Spoon the herb butter onto the paper in a broad line.

2 Fold the edge of the paper over the butter and pat down lightly. Roll the paper over the butter, squeezing it gently to form a long even roll.

3 Twist the ends of the paper like a candy wrapper, then chill the herb butter until firm.

4 Place the chicken, onions, garlic and half the tarragon in a bowl, with the orange juice. Marinate for 4 hours. Remove the chicken from the marinade. Heat 1 tablespoon oil in a frying pan. Add the onions and marinade. Cover and simmer for 15 minutes.

5 Add the sugar to the pan and cook, uncovered, for 15 minutes. Meanwhile, heat the remaining oil in another frying pan and brown the chicken. Lower the heat and cook for 10–12 minutes, turning halfway through. Place the chicken on a plate and keep hot.

6 Pour the wine into the pan. Stir well and cook until it has reduced by two-thirds. Whisk in small pieces of the butter. Add the remaining tarragon. Cook for 2–3 minutes, season and pour over the chicken breasts. Serve topped with slices of herb butter and accompanied with caramelized onions.

Port and Orange Duck with Cucumber Ribbons

Cucumber is wonderfully versatile. Here it provides an impressive garnish, worthy of this delicious orange-flavored roast duck.

Serves 4–6

INGREDIENTS
1 duck, about 5½–6 pounds
4 tablespoons red wine
2 tablespoons all-purpose flour
shredded rind and juice of 4 large oranges
¾ cup ruby port
salt and freshly ground black pepper
1 cucumber, to garnish

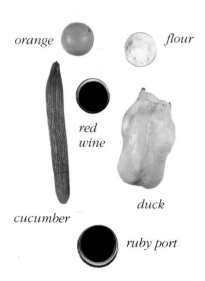

orange   *flour*

red wine

cucumber   *duck*

ruby port

COOK'S TIP
Cucumber ribbons, marinated in a little rice wine vinegar and mixed with chopped parsley, make an interesting addition to a salad.

1 Preheat the oven to 450°F. Weigh the duck and calculate the cooking time at 30 minutes per pound. Pat the duck dry. Prick the skin all over with a fork, rub in a generous amount of salt and pepper, then place the duck on a rack in a roasting pan. Roast for 15 minutes, then lower the oven temperature to 375°F and cook for the remainder of the calculated time, basting occasionally.

4 Gradually whisk in the orange juice. Simmer gently for 10 minutes.

2 Place the duck on a heated platter and let rest in a warm place for about 20 minutes. Drain the fat from the roasting pan, leaving behind the browned bits and meat juices.

5 Meanwhile make the garnish. Cut the cucumber into 2-inch lengths then cut lengthwise into quarters. Make six or seven fine horizontal cuts into the cucumber pieces, leaving ½ inch intact at one end.

3 Transfer the roasting pan to the burner. Add the red wine, stirring. Cook until the wine has almost evaporated. Sprinkle in the flour and cook, stirring, for 2–3 minutes.

6 Fold each slice over to form a loop, starting at the top and working down, until five or six loops are made. Place skin-side up on the platter with the duck. Add the port to the orange sauce and season to taste. Strain into a warm pitcher and stir in the orange rind. Serve at once with the duck.

Chicken Satay with Lime

Limes can be used in as many ways as lemons but provide more of a color contrast – particularly when mixed with cilantro.

Serves 4–6

INGREDIENTS
4 skinless, boneless chicken
  breasts
2 limes and 4–6 cilantro sprigs,
  to garnish

FOR THE MARINADE
1 small onion, finely chopped
1 tablespoon finely grated or
  crushed fresh ginger
1 tablespoon crushed garlic
2 tablespoons dark soy sauce
2 teaspoons ground coriander
1 teaspoon ground cumin
1 tablespoon dark brown sugar
1 tablespoon sunflower oil

FOR THE PEANUT DIP
½ cup smooth peanut butter
⅓ cup unsweetened
  coconut milk
2 tablespoons fish sauce
1 tablespoon fresh lime juice
dash of Tabasco sauce

1 Cut the chicken breasts into ¾ x ¼-inch strips. Combine all the marinade ingredients in a bowl, add the chicken strips and toss until coated. Cover and marinate in the fridge for 4 hours or preferably overnight.

2 Make the dip by mixing all the ingredients in a bowl. Cover and set aside for at least 1 hour to allow the flavors to combine.

3 Using a cannelle knife, cut decorative stripes lengthwise down the skin of one of the limes at ½-inch intervals, then cut the lime into ¼-inch slices. Make a cut from the center to the edge of each slice; twist to an "S" shape.

peanut butter *coconut milk* *fresh ginger* *chicken breast*

onion *dark brown sugar* *fish sauce*

ground coriander *cilantro*

limes *ground cumin* *garlic* *soy sauce*

4 Cut the remaining lime in half lengthwise and place cut-side down. Make three V-shaped cuts into the lime halves, one below the other and push each wedge out slightly to give a stepped effect. Preheat the broiler or prepare the barbecue, if using. Drain the chicken strips, reserving the marinade. Thread onto wooden skewers.

5 Either cook in a hot frying pan, place under a broiler or barbecue over moderately hot coals until tender, turning frequently and brushing occasionally with the reserved marinade. Serve garnished with the limes and cilantro sprigs. Accompany with the peanut dip.

Spicy Tomato Tart with Tomato Roses

Serve this chili-flavored tomato tart hot or cold. Echo the theme with tomato roses.

Serves 8 – 10

INGREDIENTS
2¾ cups self-rising flour
scant 1 cup butter, diced
3–4 tablespoons cold water
salt and freshly ground black
  pepper

FOR THE FILLING
2 tablespoons olive oil
2 onions, thinly sliced
1 garlic clove, crushed
6 large tomatoes, peeled
  and chopped
2 dried chilies, seeded and
  chopped
½ cup strained tomatoes
2 tablespoons superfine sugar

FOR THE GARNISH
3 firm tomatoes
sprig of basil

onion

self-rising flour

basil

strained tomatoes

butter *dried chilies*

tomatoes *garlic*

1 Process the flour, salt and butter together in a food processor or blender until they resemble bread crumbs. Add the water and process for another 5–10 seconds to mix together. Turn out onto a floured work surface and knead lightly to a firm dough. Wrap in clear film and chill. Preheat the oven to 375°F.

4 Pour the tomato sauce into the pastry shell, spreading it out evenly. Return the tomato tart to the oven for 20–25 minutes.

2 Make the filling. Heat the olive oil in a large frying pan, add the onions and garlic and fry for 10 minutes. Stir in the chopped tomatoes and chilies. Bring to a boil, lower the heat and simmer for 20–25 minutes until thickened. Add the strained tomatoes and sugar and simmer for 5 minutes more. Add salt and pepper to taste and let cool.

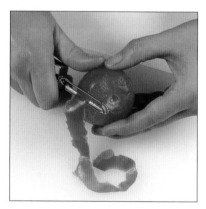

5 Meanwhile, make the garnish. Using a swivel-blade peeler and starting at the base of one of the tomatoes, peel it in one long continuous strip. Work carefully and slowly to avoid breaking the strip, and keep the peel as thin as possible. Reserve the peeled tomato for use in a soup or sauce.

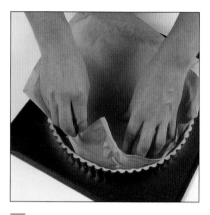

3 On a lightly floured surface, roll out the pastry and line a deep 10-inch quiche pan. Prick the base of the pastry, line with parchment paper and fill with baking beans. Bake blind for 15 minutes, then remove the beans and parchment. Return the pastry shell to the oven for 5 minutes more.

6 With the skin side out, and starting at the stem end, coil the peel loosely to within ¾ inch of the end. Set the coil upright so that it resembles a rosebud and tuck the end loosely underneath. Repeat with the remaining tomatoes. Serve the tomato tart hot or at room temperature. Garnish with the tomato roses and the basil sprig.

Noodles with Lemongrass, Chilies and Herbs

Traditional Thai ingredients provide a colorful contrast to a tasty noodle stew.

Serves 6

INGREDIENTS
2 tablespoons sunflower oil
1 onion, thickly sliced
1 lemongrass stem, finely chopped
1 tablespoon Thai red curry paste
3 zucchini, thickly sliced
1 cup Savoy cabbage, thickly sliced
2 carrots, thickly sliced
5 ounces broccoli, stem sliced thickly and head separated into florets
2 x 14-ounce cans unsweetened coconut milk
2 cups vegetable stock
5 ounces egg noodles
1 tablespoon Thai fish sauce
2 tablespoons soy sauce
4 tablespoons chopped fresh cilantro

FOR THE GARNISH
2 lemongrass stems
1 bunch cilantro
8–10 small red chilies

egg noodles
carrots

soy sauce
Savoy cabbage
lemongrass
broccoli
zucchini
cilantro
coconut milk
Thai red curry paste
onion
Thai fish sauce
red chilies

1 Heat the oil in a large saucepan or wok. Add the onion, lemongrass and Thai red curry paste. Stirring occasionally, cook for 5–10 minutes until the onion has softened.

2 Add the zucchini, cabbage, carrots and broccoli stem. Using two spoons, toss all the vegetables with the onion mixture and cook gently for about 5 minutes more.

3 Stir in the coconut milk and vegetable stock and bring to a boil. Add the noodles and the broccoli florets, lower the heat and simmer gently for 20 minutes.

4 Meanwhile, make the garnish. Split the lemongrass lengthwise through the root. Gather the cilantro into a small bouquet and lay it on a platter, following the curve of the rim.

5 Tuck the lemongrass halves into the bouquet and add the chilies to resemble flowers. Stir the fish sauce, soy sauce and chopped cilantro into the noodle mixture. Spoon onto the platter, taking care not to disturb the herb bouquet.

Creamy Risotto with Asparagus

Fine asparagus spears look great gathered in a bundle and tied with a scallion stem.

Serves 4

INGREDIENTS
6 cups vegetable stock
2 tablespoons olive oil
1 onion, finely chopped
2 garlic cloves, crushed
1 generous cup arborio rice
⅔ cup white wine
½ bunch asparagus spears, trimmed and cut into 1-inch pieces
4 tablespoons butter
3 tablespoons freshly grated Parmesan cheese

FOR THE GARNISH
12 slender asparagus spears
4 long green scallion stems, wilted

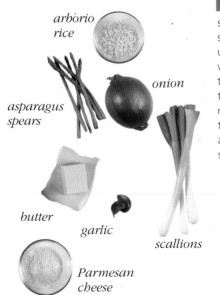

arborio rice

asparagus spears

onion

butter

garlic

scallions

olive oil

white wine

Parmesan cheese

1 Heat the stock to simmering point in a saucepan. In a separate, large pan, heat the olive oil and fry the onion and garlic for 10 minutes until softened but not colored. Add the rice, stir to coat the grains in oil and cook for 2–3 minutes. Pour in the white wine and cook until absorbed.

2 Ladle in about a quarter of the hot stock. Lower the heat to a gentle simmer and cook, stirring frequently, until it has all been absorbed. Repeat with another ladleful of stock, adding the chopped asparagus at the same time and continuing to stir. Add the remaining stock in the same way, each time allowing all the stock to be absorbed before adding more. This should take 20–25 minutes.

3 Meanwhile, make the garnish. Cook the asparagus in boiling lightly salted water until tender, then drain. Place two asparagus spears together, positioning one ¾ inch below the other. Tie the spears together with a wilted scallion stem. Make three more asparagus bundles in the same way.

4 Trim the base of each pair of spears across at an angle. Trim the ends of the scallion ties neatly. Stir the butter and Parmesan into the risotto and serve at once, garnishing each portion with an asparagus bundle.

Warm Fava Bean Salad with Filo Stars

Shelling fava beans is time-consuming but worth it for the beautiful color. Serve this delectable warm salad with spicy filo stars.

Serves 6

INGREDIENTS
2 pounds shelled fava beans
2 tablespoons olive oil
1 red onion, finely diced
2 garlic cloves, crushed
1 zucchini, finely diced
¾ cup frozen or drained
   canned corn
4 tomatoes, peeled, seeded and
   finely chopped
salt and freshly ground black
   pepper

FOR THE GARNISH
3 filo pastry sheets
1 tablespoon sunflower oil
1 teaspoon mild chili powder

corn

chili powder

olive oil

fava beans

zucchini

filo pastry

garlic

red onion

tomato

sunflower oil

1 Preheat the oven to 400°F. Bring a saucepan of water to a boil and blanch the fava beans for 2–3 minutes. Drain the beans, then refresh under cold running water and drain again. Pop the beans out of their skins and set them aside.

2 Heat the oil in a saucepan. Fry the onion and garlic gently until soft but not brown. Add the zucchini and corn and cook for 10 minutes. Add the tomatoes and fava beans and cook for 2 minutes. Season and keep warm.

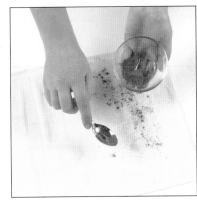

3 Make the garnish. Lay out a sheet of filo pastry. Brush lightly with the oil. Sprinkle with a third of the chili powder. Place another sheet of filo pastry on top and repeat. Repeat with the remaining sheet of filo pastry.

4 Using a large star cutter, stamp out six stars from the layered filo. Transfer them to a lightly oiled baking sheet and bake for 7–8 minutes, until golden and crisp. Serve the warm salad topped with the spicy filo stars.

Fennel Ravioli with Tartan Jackets

This ravioli has its own built-in garnish! Colored stripes, rolled into the pasta, make this dish a real show-stopper!

Serves 4–6

INGREDIENTS

FOR THE PLAIN PASTA
2 cups white bread flour
2 extra large eggs
1 extra large egg yolk
1 tablespoon olive oil

FOR THE TOMATO PASTA
1½ cups white bread flour
1 extra large egg
1 extra large egg yolk
2 tablespoons tomato paste

FOR THE SPINACH PASTA
1½ cups white bread flour
1 extra large egg
1 extra large egg yolk
1 tablespoon spinach paste

FOR THE FILLING AND GARNISH
½ cup butter
1 large fennel bulb
2 garlic cloves, crushed
½ cup heavy cream
7 ounces Gorgonzola cheese, crumbled
salt and freshly ground black pepper

COOK'S TIP

Not all the ravioli need to have tartan jackets – leaving most of them plain and making just two tartan ravioli per person can be equally effective.

fennel

white bread flour

Gorgonzola cheese

spinach

olive oil

eggs

heavy cream

1 Place the flour, eggs, egg yolk and olive oil for the plain pasta, in a food processor or blender and process until the dough forms a ball around the blade. If dry, add a little water. Knead briefly until smooth, place in a bowl, cover and let rest for an hour. Repeat with the tomato pasta ingredients and then with the spinach pasta ingredients.

2 Make the filling. Heat the butter in a frying pan. Set aside the fennel fronds to sprinkle over each serving, then dice the fennel bulb. Add to the pan with the garlic, cover and let sweat gently for 10 minutes until tender. Stir in the cream and cheese. Cook for 5 minutes, season to taste and set aside to cool.

3 Divide the plain dough into small pieces and pass through a pasta machine, reducing the roller settings until the sheets are medium-thin. Place the finished sheets on a baking sheet dusted with flour and cover with a damp cloth and clear plastic to prevent it from drying out while you prepare the other pasta in the same way. On the final rolling, cut both the tomato and the spinach dough into fettucine (strips about ½-inch wide).

4 Return one piece of plain pasta to the pasta machine. Place strips of spinach pasta lengthwise down the sheet in parallel rows and roll through the machine. Place back in the machine and repeat the process with strips of tomato pasta, this time placing them across the pasta sheet to give a tartan effect. Pass the pasta through the machine several times, each time reducing the thickness until fairly thin. Make more tartan sheets, as required, in the same way.

5 Place a finished sheet of pasta, on a lightly floured work surface. Cut into 2½-inch squares. Brush lightly with a little water. Place a teaspoon of the fennel mixture in the center of each pasta square.

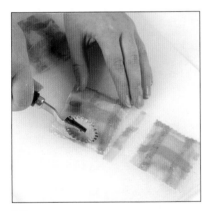

6 Cut a second sheet of pasta into squares of the same size and place on top of the filled squares. Crimp the edges of each square with a fork or use a crimping wheel. Bring a large pan of lightly salted water to a boil. Cook the ravioli in batches for 5 minutes or until they rise to the surface of the water. Drain well and serve, garnished with the reserved fennel fronds.

Roast Peppers and Zucchini

Colorful tomato suns complement a broiled mixed pepper salad.

Serves 4

INGREDIENTS
2 red bell peppers, quartered
   and seeded
2 yellow bell peppers, quartered
   and seeded
2 zucchini
3 tablespoons olive oil
1 tablespoon white wine
   vinegar
2 tablespoons chopped fresh
   cilantro
salt and freshly ground black
   pepper

FOR THE GARNISH
8 red cherry tomatoes

cilantro

zucchini

red and yellow
bell peppers

cherry
tomatoes

olive
oil

white wine
vinegar

1 Preheat the broiler to medium. Put the peppers flesh-side down on a foil-lined broiler pan and broil for about 10–15 minutes until blackened and soft. Place in a plastic bag, close tightly and let cool. Peel off the skin and cut the pepper flesh into ½-inch strips.

2 Using a swivel-blade peeler, cut the zucchini into ribbons. Heat 1 table-spoon of the olive oil in a frying pan, and sauté the zucchini for 2–3 minutes. Place in a bowl with the peppers. Whisk together the remaining oil, vinegar and cilantro. Pour over the vegetables, season and toss lightly.

3 Make the garnish. Place a tomato stem-side down. Cut lightly into the skin across the top, edging the knife down toward the base on either side. Turn the tomato through 90 degrees and repeat, turning and cutting until the skin has been cut into eight separate segments, joined at the base.

4 Carefully slide the top of the knife under the point of each segment and ease the skin away toward the base, stopping just short. Gently fold the petals back to mimic the sun's rays. Make more suns in the same way. Spoon the salad onto individual plates, adding two tomato suns to each.

Creamy Pasta with Parmesan Curls

Several perfectly formed curls of Parmesan give a plate of creamy pasta a lift.

Serves 4–6

INGREDIENTS
9 ounces dried campanelle
   pasta
2 tablespoons olive oil
1¼ cups mascarpone cheese
scant 1 cup sour cream
¾ cup freshly grated Parmesan
   cheese
4 ounces sun-dried tomatoes
   in oil, drained and thinly
   sliced
salt and freshly ground black
   pepper

FOR THE GARNISH
1 piece of Parmesan cheese,
   about 6 ounces

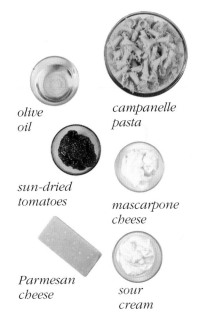

olive oil

campanelle pasta

sun-dried tomatoes

mascarpone cheese

Parmesan cheese

sour cream

1 Unless you are an old hand at making Parmesan curls, do this first, before cooking the pasta. Holding a swivel-blade peeler at a 45-degree angle, roll it steadily across the chunk of Parmesan cheese to form a curl. Make several curls, depending on the number of guests being served.

2 Bring a large saucepan of lightly salted water to a boil. Add the olive oil and pasta, stir and cook according to the instructions on the package.

3 Meanwhile, melt the mascarpone and sour cream together in a separate saucepan. Add the Parmesan and sun-dried tomatoes and cook over low heat for 5 minutes. Season with plenty of black pepper and a little salt.

4 Drain the pasta, return it to the pan and pour the sauce over the top. Toss to mix together thoroughly. Serve on individual plates, adding a few Parmesan curls to each portion.

Eggplant Parmesan with Leek Haystacks

Stacks of deep-fried golden shreds of leek look delicious served with this Mediterranean dish.

Serves 4–6

INGREDIENTS
2 x 14-ounce cans chopped
  tomatoes
1 teaspoon white wine vinegar
1 tablespoon superfine sugar
2 tablespoons pesto
3 eggplants
6 tablespoons olive oil
butter, for greasing
12 ounces mozzarella cheese,
  thinly sliced
3 tablespoons fresh bread
  crumbs
¼ cup freshly grated Parmesan
  cheese
salt and freshly ground black
  pepper

FOR THE GARNISH
1 large leek
2 tablespoons all-purpose flour
oil, for deep-frying

olive oil

Parmesan cheese

bread crumbs

mozzarella cheese

pesto

chopped tomatoes

eggplant

white wine vinegar

leek

1 Pour the canned tomatoes into a saucepan. Bring to a boil, then simmer for 20 minutes. Purée in a blender or food processor. Return to the pan and add the vinegar, sugar, pesto, and seasoning. Cook for 5 minutes, then remove the pan from the heat.

2 Cut the eggplants lengthwise into ¼-inch thick slices. Heat 2 tablespoons of the oil in a large frying pan. Fry the eggplant, in batches, for 5–6 minutes until golden, turning once and adding more oil as required. Drain well on paper towels.

3 Preheat the oven to 400°F. Butter a large shallow baking dish. Lay a third of the eggplant slices on the bottom of the dish, then spoon over a third of the tomato sauce.

4 Top with a third of the mozzarella slices. Make two more layers, using the remaining ingredients. Sprinkle the bread crumbs and Parmesan evenly over the top. Bake for 35–40 minutes until golden and bubbling.

5 Meanwhile make the garnish. Slice the leek lengthwise in half and then into quarters. Cut into 2-inch lengths and then into very fine julienne. Place in a mixing bowl, sprinkle with flour and toss to coat.

6 Just before the eggplant is ready, heat the oil to 325°F. Drop small spoonfuls of the floured leeks into the oil and cook for 30–45 seconds until golden. Drain on paper towels. Repeat with the remaining leeks. Serve the eggplant with a small stack of leeks on top of each portion.

Port Wine Gelatin Dessert with Trailed Cream Hearts

There can be few more impressive desserts than this – a rich black currant coulis swirled with hearts surrounds a sophisticated gelatin dessert.

Serves 6–8

INGREDIENTS
6 sheets of leaf gelatin
2 cups water
4 cups black currants
1 cup superfine sugar
⅔ cup ruby port
2 tablespoons crème de cassis
½ cup light cream, to decorate

light cream

ruby port

black currants

leaf gelatin

superfine sugar

crème de cassis

COOK'S TIP

If you have trouble finding leaf gelatin it can be substituted with powdered gelatin. Use 1 teaspoon for each gelatin leaf, and simply sprinkle over the port at the beginning of step 2.

1 In a small bowl, soak the gelatin in 5 tablespoons of the water until soft. Place the black currants, sugar and 1¼ cups of the remaining water in a large saucepan. Bring to a boil, lower the heat and simmer for 20 minutes. Strain, reserving the cooking liquid in a large pitcher. Put half the black currants in a bowl and pour over 4 tablespoons of the reserved cooking liquid. (Freeze the remaining black currants for later use.) Set the bowl and pitcher aside.

2 Squeeze the water out of the gelatin and place in a small saucepan with the port, cassis and remaining water. Heat gently to dissolve the gelatin but do not allow the mixture to boil. Stir into the pitcher of black currant liquid until well mixed.

4 Run a fine knife around each dessert. Dip each mold in hot water for 5–10 seconds, then turn the dessert out onto your hand. Place on a plate and spoon the coulis around.

3 Run six to eight ring molds under cold water, drain and place in a roasting pan. Fill with the port mixture. Chill for at least 6 hours until set. Turn the bowl of black currants into a food processor or blender, purée until smooth, then pass through a fine strainer. Taste the coulis and adjust the sweetness.

5 Drop a little cream at intervals onto the coulis. Drag a toothpick through the cream dots, dragging each one in turn into a heart shape. Serve the desserts immediately.

Raspberry Sorbet with a Berry Garland

This stunning fresh fruit and herb garnish creates a bold border for the scoops of sorbet.

Serves 6–8

INGREDIENTS
¾ cup superfine sugar
1 cup water
2⅔ cups fresh or thawed
   frozen raspberries
strained juice of 1 orange

FOR THE DECORATION
1 bunch fresh mint
selection of soft fruits,
   including strawberries,
   raspberries, red currants and
   blueberries

 raspberries

 orange   *sugar*

 red currants   *blueberries*

 mint   *strawberries*

COOK'S TIP
Make the sorbet in an ice cream maker, if you have one, following the manufacturer's instructions.

1 Heat the sugar with the water in a saucepan, until dissolved, stirring occasionally. Bring to a boil, then set aside to cool. Purée the raspberries with the orange juice in a blender or food processor, then use a wooden spoon to press through a strainer to remove any seeds.

2 Mix the syrup with the puréed raspberries and pour into a freezer container. Freeze for 2 hours or until ice crystals form around the edges. Whisk until smooth, then return to the freezer for 4 hours.

3 About 30 minutes before serving, transfer the sorbet to the fridge to soften slightly. Place a large sprig of mint on the rim of a serving plate, then build up a garland using more sprigs.

4 Leaving on the leaves, cut the strawberries in half. Arrange on the mint with the other fruit. Place the fruits at different angles and link the leaves with strings of red currants. Place scoops of sorbet in the center.

Lemon Mousse with Shortbread Hearts

Shortbread can be stamped out into any shape, baked and then lightly dusted with sugar. For a special occasion, frosted rose petals can be used as a decoration in place of the lemon rind.

Serves 6–8

INGREDIENTS
4 sheets of leaf gelatin
4 tablespoons water
1 cup mascarpone cheese
1 cup ricotta cheese
3 tablespoons confectioner's
  sugar, sifted
grated rind and juice of
  2 lemons
3 egg whites

FOR THE SHORTBREAD HEARTS
¼ cup chopped almonds,
  toasted
6 tablespoons superfine sugar
1¼ cups all-purpose flour
½ cup butter, diced
sifted confectioner's sugar,
  for dusting

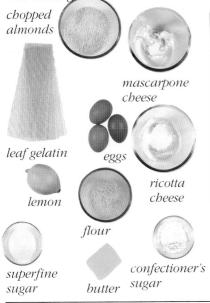

chopped almonds

mascarpone cheese

leaf gelatin

eggs

lemon

ricotta cheese

flour

superfine sugar

butter

confectioner's sugar

1 Soak the gelatin in the water until soft. Beat the mascarpone, ricotta cheese and sugar together until fluffy. Squeeze out the water from the gelatin and melt with the lemon juice in a small saucepan. Cool slightly, then beat into the mascarpone mixture.

2 Whisk the egg whites until stiff. Fold into the mascarpone mixture, with half the lemon rind. Spoon into serving dishes and chill for 3–4 hours until set.

3 Meanwhile, make the shortbread hearts. Process the almonds and sugar in a food processor or blender until fine. Add the flour and mix. Add the butter and process until a dough forms. Turn out and knead lightly. Wrap in clear plastic and chill for 20 minutes. Preheat the oven to 350°F.

4 Line a baking sheet with baking parchment. Roll out the dough on a lightly floured surface to ¼-inch thick. Stamp out heart-shaped cookies, put on the baking sheet and bake for 10–12 minutes. Cool. Dust with sugar. Top the mousse with the remaining lemon rind and serve with the hearts.

Chocolate Mousse with Chocolate Curls

Dark, white and milk chocolate curls provide a finishing flourish for a sumptuous chocolate mousse with just a hint of ginger.

Serves 6–8

INGREDIENTS
1 pound semisweet chocolate,
  finely chopped
5 tablespoons butter
scant 1 cup superfine sugar
6 eggs, separated
4 tablespoons ginger syrup
  (from a jar of preserved
  ginger)
5 tablespoons brandy

FOR THE DECORATION
4 ounces semisweet chocolate
  or a mixture of semisweet,
  milk and white chocolate

semisweet chocolate

ginger syrup

brandy

superfine sugar

eggs

butter

COOK'S TIP
The mousse can be made up to 3 days in advance, provided it is kept in the fridge.

1 Melt the chocolate and butter with half the sugar in a bowl set over a saucepan of hot water. Remove the bowl from the pan and beat in the egg yolks, ginger syrup and brandy.

2 Whisk the egg whites in a large clean bowl until soft peaks form. Gradually add the remaining sugar, a spoonful at a time, whisking constantly until stiff and glossy.

3 Beat about a third of the egg whites into the chocolate mixture to lighten it, then fold in the remainder. Pour into six or eight serving bowls or glasses and chill for 3–4 hours until set.

4 To make the chocolate curls, melt the chocolate, beat it briefly, then pour it onto a flat surface such as a baking sheet. Spread out with a metal spatula until about ⅛-inch thick. Let cool until firm but pliable.

5 For a more dramatic effect, make light and dark curls, using semisweet, milk and white chocolate. Pipe the melted chocolate in alternate rows, smooth each in turn with a metal spatula and allow to firm before making the curls.

6 Hold a cheese slicer and place flat against the chocolate. Pull it gently toward you, scraping off a thin layer of chocolate so that it curls into a scroll. Work quickly or the chocolate will harden and splinter. Decorate the mousses just before serving.

Mango Ice Cream with Exotic Fruit Salad

Exotic fruits are now widely available: choose your fruits with care, taking color, shape and taste into account, then use them to create your own still life next to a great mango and ginger ice cream.

Serves 6–8

INGREDIENTS
2 large ripe mangoes, peeled and coarsely chopped
2 pieces of preserved ginger, plus 2 tablespoons ginger syrup
1 cup heavy cream

FOR THE DECORATION
1 star fruit, thickly sliced
1 mango, peeled and cut into wedges
1 cantaloupe melon, cut into wedges
6 strawberries, cut in half
1 small bunch frosted grapes

cantaloupe melon

mangoes

grapes

ginger syrup

star fruit

heavy cream

strawberries

ginger

1 Purée the mangoes in a food processor or blender with the ginger and ginger syrup, until smooth.

2 Whip the cream in a large bowl until it forms fairly firm peaks. Fold in the mango purée.

3 Transfer to a freezer container. Freeze for 2 hours, then beat with an electric mixer until smooth. Return the ice cream to the freezer and freeze for at least 8 hours. Alternatively, freeze in an ice cream maker according to the manufacturer's instructions.

4 About 30 minutes before serving, transfer the ice cream to the fridge to soften slightly. Arrange the prepared fruit on individual plates and add two scoops of ice cream to each one.

Raspberries with a Tricolor Swirled Purée

Three fruit purées, swirled together, make a kaleidoscopic garnish for a nest of raspberries.

Serves 4–6

INGREDIENTS
generous 1 cup raspberries
½ cup red wine
confectioner's sugar, for dusting

FOR THE DECORATION
1 large mango, peeled and
   chopped
14 ounces kiwi fruit, peeled
   and chopped
generous 1 cup raspberries
confectioner's sugar, to taste

red wine

confectioner's sugar

mango

kiwi fruit

raspberries

COOK'S TIP
Purées can be prepared from any available fruit. They freeze well and are ready for making an easy last-minute garnish.

1 Place the raspberries in a bowl with the red wine and allow to macerate for about 2 hours.

2 Make the decoration. Purée the mango in a food processor or blender, adding a little water if necessary. Press through a strainer into a bowl. Purée the kiwi fruit in the same way, then make a third purée from the remaining raspberries. Sweeten the purées with sifted confectioner's sugar, if necessary.

3 Spoon each purée onto a serving plate, separating the kiwi and mango with the raspberry purée as if creating a four-wedged pie. Gently tap the plate on the work surface to settle the purées against each other.

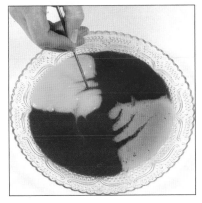

4 Using a skewer, draw a spiral outward from the center of the plate to the rim. Drain the macerated raspberries, pile them in the center, and dust them heavily with sugar.

Apricot Ice Cream under a Caramel Cage

Caramel is a favorite with confectioners because of its decorative possibilities. It is used here to create a cage to cover a tea-scented apricot ice cream.

Serves 6–8

INGREDIENTS
2 cups dried apricots
3¾ cups cold Earl Grey tea
¾ cup light brown sugar
2 tablespoons brandy or gin
  (optional)
1¼ cups whipping cream

FOR THE DECORATION
2½ cups superfine sugar
¾ cup water
½ cup liquid glucose
oil, for greasing

light brown sugar

brandy

superfine sugar

Earl Grey tea bags

liquid glucose

dried apricots

whipping cream

1 Place the apricots in a large bowl, Pour the cold Earl Grey tea over, cover and soak for 4 hours or overnight.

2 Turn the apricots and the tea into a saucepan. Add the sugar. Bring to a boil, stirring to dissolve the sugar. Simmer gently for 15–20 minutes until the apricots are tender. Allow to cool.

3 Process the apricots with the cooking liquid in a food processor or blender to a rough purée; the apricots should be chopped but still identifiable. Stir in the brandy or gin, if using.

4 Whip the cream in a large bowl until soft peaks form. Fold in the apricot purée and mix well. Transfer to a container suitable for freezing and freeze for 2 hours. Beat with an electric mixer until smooth, then return to the freezer for at least 8 hours. Or, place in an ice cream maker and freeze according to the manufacturer's instructions.

5 Meanwhile, make the decoration. Place the sugar and water in a small saucepan. Heat gently, stirring until the sugar dissolves. Bring to a boil and add the liquid glucose. Cook until the mixture is a pale caramel. Cool slightly. Lightly oil the back of a ladle.

6 Using a teaspoon, trail caramel over the ladle in horizontal and vertical lines, until a "cage" is built. Let harden, then gently ease off. Repeat with the remaining caramel, reheating if necessary, to make six to eight "cages". To serve, set a cage over scoops of ice cream.

Chocolate Grapevine with Chocolate Leaves

Few people can resist a chocolate truffle and this provides a perfect chance to show off with home-made truffles made to look like a bunch of grapes, with chocolate branches and leaves.

Makes 30–40 truffles

INGREDIENTS
1 pound semisweet chocolate, chopped
4 tablespoons butter
¾ cup heavy cream
1 pound milk chocolate

FOR THE DECORATION
4 ounces semisweet chocolate, melted
oil, for brushing
4 rose leaves, washed and dried

milk chocolate

semisweet chocolate

butter

heavy cream

COOK'S TIP

Leaves that are nicely shaped and shiny, with well-defined veins, make the best chocolate leaves. Holly works well, as do rose leaves, but avoid any poisonous leaves.

1 Melt the semisweet chocolate and butter in a bowl set over a pan of hot water. Place the cream in another bowl and whisk until firm peaks form. Fold the cream into the chocolate mixture, cover and chill for 4–5 hours until firm.

2 Using a melon baller dipped in hot water, scoop the chocolate mixture into balls. Place on a sheet of waxed paper.

3 Grate half the milk chocolate onto a sheet of waxed paper and melt the remainder. Dip each truffle in melted chocolate then roll in grated chocolate. Allow to set. Arrange the truffles on a dish to resemble a bunch of grapes.

4 Make the decoration. Use a little melted dark chocolate to pipe a "Y" onto waxed paper. Chill until set. Peel off the paper gently and place the "Y" at the top of the bunch of truffles.

5 Very lightly oil the leaves, then brush them with the remaining melted dark chocolate to make a coating at least ⅛-inch thick. Chill until set.

6 Carefully peel the real leaves away from the chocolate. Using a tiny dot of melted chocolate, stick the chocolate leaves to the branch.

Poached Pears with Cinnamon Stacks

Stacks of cinnamon sticks make an attractive addition to a plate – simply tie them together with gold ribbon.

Serves 6

INGREDIENTS
6 eating pears
3 cups ruby port
7 tablespoons superfine sugar
2 cinnamon sticks

FOR THE DECORATION
36 cinnamon sticks
6 gold ribbons, each
   12 inches long

ruby port

superfine sugar

cinnamon sticks

pears

gold ribbons

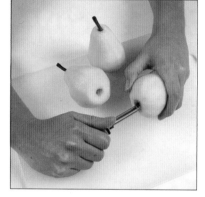

1 Peel the pears, leaving the stalks intact. Push the end of a swivel-blade vegetable peeler into the base of each pear to a depth of about 1½ inches. Twist and remove the core.

2 Slice ¼ inch off the bottom of each pear so that it will stand upright. Stand the pears in a saucepan that will hold them comfortably but snugly. Add the port, sugar and cinnamon sticks.

3 Bring the port to a boil, cover, lower the heat and simmer for about 15–20 minutes until the pears are tender. Transfer the pears to a dish and keep hot. Boil the port syrup until reduced by half.

4 Meanwhile, make the decoration. Gather the cinnamon sticks together in bundles of six.

5 Tie a length of ribbon around the center of each bundle. Finish in a bow and trim the ends of the ribbon into a point. Stand the pears in individual bowls, pour a little of the port syrup over and decorate the rim of each bowl with a stack of cinnamon sticks.

COOK'S TIP
Try to use long cinnamon sticks for this garnish – they look far more attractive than shorter ones. Look out for them in delis and Asian stores.

Pavlova Roulade with Cream Swirls

Soft swirls of cream and strawberries make a pretty decoration for this meltingly light meringue.

Serves 8–10

INGREDIENTS
1 teaspoon vanilla extract
1 teaspoon cornstarch
1 teaspoon white wine vinegar
5 egg whites
scant 1½ cups superfine sugar
1⅔ cups heavy cream
¾ cup ricotta cheese
3 tablespoons confectioner's
sugar, sifted
1 tablespoon lemon juice
2 tablespoons grated lemon rind
1½ cups strawberries, thinly
sliced

FOR THE DECORATION
¾ cup strawberries
½ cup heavy cream
confectioner's sugar, for dusting

confectioner's
sugar

white wine
vinegar

heavy
cream

superfine sugar

vanilla
extract

strawberries

ricotta cheese

eggs

lemon

1 Preheat the oven to 300°F. Line the base and sides of a 13 x 9 inch jelly roll pan with non-stick parchment paper. Mix the vanilla extract, cornstarch and vinegar in a small bowl and set aside.

2 Whisk the egg whites until soft peaks form. Add the superfine sugar, a spoonful at a time, whisking constantly until the mixture is stiff and glossy. Whisk in the cornstarch mixture before adding the final spoonful of sugar. Spoon into the pan and spread over evenly. Bake for 25 minutes.

3 Dust a sheet of waxed paper with confectioner's sugar. Invert the meringue onto the paper, peel off the lining paper, cover lightly and cool. Whip the cream until soft peaks form. Fold in the ricotta cheese, sugar, lemon juice and rind and spread over the meringue to within ½ inch of the edges.

4 Sprinkle the sliced strawberries evenly over the cream. Then, using the waxed paper underneath as a guide, roll the meringue up from one long edge. Transfer to a serving plate and dust with confectioner's sugar.

5 To decorate, cut the strawberries in half lengthwise, then into quarters, without removing any leaves. Whip the cream and spoon it into a pastry bag fitted with a star tip.

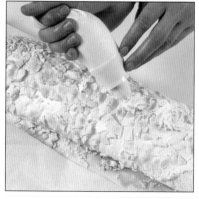

6 Pipe swirls of cream at intervals along the top of the roll – these can be used as portion guides. Top each swirl with a strawberry quarter. Dust each serving with confectioner's sugar, if desired, and serve.

Blackberry and Apple Pie with a Pastry Rose

Pastry is perfect for shaping – here roses and leaves are used to decorate a special fruit pie.

Serves 8–10

INGREDIENTS
2¼ cups all-purpose flour
½ cup confectioner's sugar, sifted
scant 1 cup unsalted butter, diced
1 egg yolk
1–2 tablespoons cold water
beaten egg, for glazing

FOR THE FILLING
1 pound cooking apples
2 tablespoons water
1 pound blackberries
3 tablespoons crème de cassis
sugar, to taste

cooking apples   *flour*

blackberries   *sugar*

butter   *egg*

crème de cassis

1 Preheat the oven to 375°F. Place the flour, sugar and butter in a food processor or blender and process until the mixture resembles coarse bread-crumbs. Add the egg yolk and enough water to bind the dough. Process for 5–10 seconds. Knead lightly on a floured surface. Wrap and chill.

2 Quarter, peel, core and chop the apples. Place in a saucepan with the water, cover and cook over low heat until cooked to a fluffy pulp. Add the blackberries and cook for 5 minutes more, then stir in the cassis and sugar to taste. Remove from the heat.

3 Pinch off one-sixth of the pastry and set it aside. Divide the rest in half. Roll out one piece to a large circle and use to line a deep 8-inch pie dish. Spoon in the blackberry and apple mixture, then roll out a top from the second large piece of pastry and cover the filling. Crimp the edges of the pie.

4 Roll out the remaining pastry thinly. Cut two strips, one 4 x ¾ inches, and the other 5 x 1 inches. Loosely roll up each strip, pinching together occasionally. Pinch the bases and shape into roses.

5 Cut two 5 x ¼-inch strips for stems. Cut 2-inch leaf shapes out of the remaining pastry and draw on veins with a sharp knife.

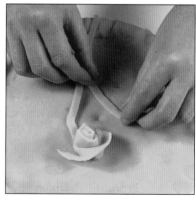

6 Brush the pie with a little water and arrange the roses, stems and leaves on top. Brush the pastry top and decora-tion with beaten egg. Bake for 30 minutes until golden. Serve hot or cold.

Chocolate Almond Cake with Chocolate-dipped Fruit

Chocolate-dipped physalis and strawberries create a perfect partnership for this gorgeous chocolate cake.

Serves 8–10

INGREDIENTS
9 ounces semisweet chocolate, chopped
½ cup butter, plus extra for greasing
4 eggs, separated
scant ½ cup superfine sugar
1 cup ground almonds
4 tablespoons brandy, rum or Madeira

FOR THE DECORATION
8 physalis
2 ounces semisweet chocolate, melted
8 strawberries
cocoa powder, for dusting

chocolate

ground almonds

eggs

brandy

superfine sugar

butter

strawberries

physalis

1 Preheat the oven to 350°F. Grease and line the bottom of a shallow 10-inch round cake pan. Melt the chocolate and butter together in a large heatproof bowl. In a separate bowl, whisk the egg yolks with half of the sugar until thick and pale.

2 Whisk the egg yolks into the chocolate mixture. Fold in the ground almonds and brandy, rum or Madeira.

3 Whisk the egg whites in a large clean bowl until soft peaks form. Gradually add the remaining sugar, a spoonful at a time, continuing to whisk constantly until the mixture is stiff and glossy. Beat one-third into the chocolate mixture, then fold in the rest.

4 Pour into the pan and tap it sharply on the work surface to remove any air bubbles. Bake for 40 minutes or until a fine skewer inserted in the cake comes out clean. Invert onto a cake board or plate, placed on a wire rack. Allow to cool – the cake should sink slightly.

5 Make the decoration. Tear open the papery husks of the physalis and twist back to form a little umbrella. Have ready a sheet of non-stick parchment paper on a baking sheet.

6 Holding a physalis by the husks, half dip the fruit in the melted chocolate. Put on the non-stick parchment paper to set. Repeat with the strawberries. Dust the cake with cocoa. Serve the cake decorated with the dipped fruit.

Crêpes with Oranges and Meringue Crests

Meringue crests appear as perfect pinnacles on top of delicate crêpes filled with tangy oranges.

Serves 6–8

INGREDIENTS
1 cup all-purpose flour
1 tablespoon superfine sugar
pinch of salt
1 egg
1¼ cups milk
4 tablespoons butter, melted
oil, for frying
2 egg whites
4 tablespoons superfine sugar
grated rind of orange, to decorate

FOR THE FILLING
4 tablespoons butter
4 oranges, peeled and
  segmented
½ cup confectioner's sugar,
  sifted
2 tablespoons Cointreau or
  other orange-flavored liqueur

superfine sugar

flour

oranges

milk

eggs *butter*

Cointreau

confectioner's sugar

1 Preheat the oven to 400°F. Sift the flour, sugar and salt into a mixing bowl. Beat the egg into the milk in a pitcher or bowl, then gradually whisk into the flour to form a smooth batter. Whisk in the melted butter.

2 Heat a little oil in a crêpe pan or small frying pan. Pour in a thin layer of batter, tilting to coat the pan. Cook for 20–25 seconds until golden underneath. Flip and cook for 10–15 seconds. Make more crêpes in the same way.

3 Wipe the pan with paper towels and melt the butter. When it starts to bubble, add the orange segments and sugar. Cook for 5 minutes, stirring occasionally. Add the liqueur and warm through. Remove and keep warm.

4 Whisk the egg whites in a clean bowl until soft peaks form. Add the sugar, a spoonful at a time, whisking constantly until stiff and glossy. Spoon into a pastry bag fitted with a star tip.

5 Line a baking sheet with non-stick parchment paper. Fold a crêpe in half. Spoon several orange segments and a little sauce on one half, then fold over to make a triangular shape enclosing the filling. Place on the prepared baking sheet. Fill the remaining crêpes in the same way.

6 Pipe a row of meringue shells down the center of each pancake triangle. Bake for 5–6 minutes until the meringue is golden. Serve at once with the remaining sauce, decorated with the orange rind.

INDEX